IDIOMS ARE FUN!

Learning about idioms is like going on a treasure hunt for secret messages! Idioms are phrases that have a special meaning beyond the regular words used. It's like when you and your friends have a secret code language, idioms are similar but used by everyone in a language. By learning idioms, you'll understand more about the way people talk and be able to express yourself in a fun and creative way.

In this book, you'll discover 100 of the most popular and interesting idiomatic expressions used in the English language. From classic sayings to more contemporary expressions, this book is a treasure trove of linguistic gems. Whether you're a native speaker or learning English as a second language, you'll find this book to be an enjoyable and educational read. So, sit back, relax, and join us on a journey through the world of idioms.

CONTENTS

SILENCE SPEAKS VOLUMES

What does it mean?

When someone is quiet and doesn't say anything, it can tell us a lot about what they're thinking or feeling. Just like when we speak, our silence can also speak for us.

Where does it come from?

People have been saying this phrase for a long time, but no one is exactly sure where it came from.

How to use it?

When the classroom got quiet during the teacher's question, it was clear that the students didn't know the answer. Their silence spoke volumes.

TO BARK UP THE WRONG TREE

What does it mean?

If you bark up the wrong tree, it means you're looking for something in the wrong place. It's like when a dog barks at a tree because it thinks there's a squirrel there, but there's actually nothing there.

Where does it come from?

This idiom comes from early 1800s when people used to hunt with dogs. They would try to catch animals like raccoons, but sometimes the animals would trick the dogs. If the dogs thought the animal was in a tree, but it wasn't really there, the dogs were "barking up the wrong tree."

How to use it?

When Tommy thought his little sister took his toy, he started shouting at her. But it turns out she didn't do it. He was barking up the wrong tree.

BULL IN A CHINA SHOP

What does it mean?

A bull in a china shop is someone who is not careful and breaks things. It's like if a big, strong bull went into a store that sells delicate things made of china and broke them all by accident.

Where does it come from?

A long time ago, people started using the phrase "like a bull in a china shop" to describe someone who is not careful and breaks things. Other languages have similar phrases with an elephant, but in English, we use a bull.

How to use it?

When Johnny played soccer in the house, he knocked over a vase and broke it. He was like a bull in a china shop.

TO BREAK A LEG

What does it mean?

When people say "break a leg," they're trying to wish you good luck. It's kind of like saying "do your best." Even though it sounds like you might get hurt, it's actually a nice thing to say.

Where does it come from?

Some people think it started in old theaters, where actors would bow and try to break a leg of the furniture on stage. Others think it was because if the performance was so good, the audience would stand up and "break" their legs from being so into the show.

How to use it?

"Good luck on your spelling bee today, Sarah! I hope you get all the words right. Break a leg!"

TO CALL IT A DAY

What does it mean?

When people say "let's call it a day," they mean it's time to stop working or playing and take a rest. It's like saying, "Okay, we've done enough for now, let's go have some fun!"

Where does it come from?

This idiom is thought to have originated from farms or in factories, where they would literally call out to signal the end of the workday. It could also come from the idea of "calling in the day," as in declaring or acknowledging that the day has ended.

How to use it?

"It's getting late, kids. Let's pack up our toys and call it a day. It's time for bed."

TO BITE THE BULLET

What does it mean?

When people say they need to "bite the bullet," it means they're going to do something that's hard or uncomfortable.

Where does it come from?

A long time ago, when soldiers got hurt in a war, they had to have surgery without medicine to help them not feel the pain. To make it easier, they would bite down on a bullet so they wouldn't cry out.

How to use it?

"I don't like broccoli, but it's good for me. I'll just have to bite the bullet and eat it."

TO COST AN ARM AND A LEG

What does it mean?

When people say that something costs an arm and a leg, it means that it's really expensive.

Where does it come from?

In 1600s people in Ireland used coins called halfpennies. Two men named Armstrong and Legge were allowed to make these coins. The idiom came from their names, and initially it was used to say something was going to cost you a halfpenny.

How to use it?

"Mom, can I buy that toy? It looks so cool!" "I'm sorry honey, but it costs an arm and a leg. We'll have to find something else."

TO BEND OVER BACKWARDS

What does it mean?

When people say "to bend over backwards," they mean that someone is trying very hard to do something or help someone else. It's like when you bend over backwards to reach for something, you are using all your effort and doing whatever it takes to get it.

Where does it come from?

This idiom comes from gymnastics. A long time ago, people used this term to describe when someone had to stretch and bend their back a lot in order to do something really well.

How to use it?

Samantha wanted to make sure her best friend had the best birthday party, so she bent over backwards to plan everything just right.

TO BURY THE HATCHET

What does it mean?

When people say "to bury the hatchet," they mean to put aside differences and make peace with someone after an argument or conflict. It's like when two friends who fought with each other finally make up and become friends again.

Where does it come from?

The phrase comes from the Native American tradition of burying a hatchet to symbolize the end of a conflict and the start of peace.

How to use it?

"Me and my best friend had a fight but we buried the hatchet and now we're playing together again."

TO CRY OVER SPILT MILK

What does it mean?

When people say "to cry over spilt milk," they mean to be upset about something that has already happened and cannot be changed.

Where does it come from?

This idiom is the contemporary version of "No weeping for shed milk" originally published in 1659 in a book of proverbs by Welsh historian and author James Howell.

How to use it?

"I know you're disappointed that your toy is broken, but there is no point crying over spilled milk. Let's buy a new one when we go to the shop."

PIECE OF CAKE

What does it mean?

The idiom "piece of cake" means something that is very easy to do or accomplish.

Where does it come from?

In the 1930s, people in the British Royal Air Force used this saying to talk about a flying missions that were so simple, it was like eating a piece of cake - which is a treat that's easy and enjoyable to have.

How to use it?

"Don't worry about the test tomorrow, it's going to be a piece of cake!"

EASIER SAID THAN DONE

What does it mean?

This idiom is often used to express that something sounds simple in theory, but is much more challenging in practice.

Where does it come from?

The saying "easier said than done" has been around for a long time, and was first written down in a book from 1483. The book was written in old language and said "It is easyer to saye than to do."

How to use it?

"I want to learn a new language, but studying every day is easier said than done."

TO HIT THE NAIL ON THE HEAD

What does it mean?

When people "hit the nail on the head," they are doing or saying exactly what is needed in a situation. It means that they are exactly right or accurate in their understanding or action.

Where does it come from?

This idiom comes from carpentry, where you have to hit a nail in just the right spot to make it go into the wood.

How to use it?

"You figured out what was wrong with the toy, you really hit the nail on the head!"

TO KEEP AN EYE OUT

What does it mean?

When you "keep an eye out" for something, it means you are paying attention and looking for it. It can mean that you are keeping watch or being careful to notice something, especially if it's important or needs your attention.

Where does it come from?

It is a common expression that has been in use for many years, and likely comes from the idea of keeping watch or being vigilant in order to see something important. The use of the word "eye" in this context means to pay attention or look for something.

How to use it?

"I've lost my glasses again.
Can you keep an eye out for them? "

THE LIGHTS ARE ON BUT NOBODY'S HOME

What does it mean?

This idiom means that someone appears to be awake and alert, but is actually not paying attention or understanding what's going on.

Where does it come from?

The origins of this idiom are unclear, but it has been in use since at least 1980s.

How to use it?

"I asked Johnny a question, but it was like the lights were on but nobody's home. He just stared at me without answering."

WHEN PIGS FLY

What does it mean?

When people say "when pigs fly," they usually mean that the thing they're talking about is never going to happen, no matter how much time goes by.

Where does it come from?

The first known use of the phrase "when pigs fly" comes from English lexicographer John Withals, who wrote it down in a Latin-English dictionary in 1616. Withal wrote "pigs fly in the ayre with their tayles forward", implying the impossibility not only of the flight of pigs but also backwards flight.

How to use it?

"Will the kids ever clean their room without being told? That'll happen when pigs fly!"

TO WOLF DOWN

What does it mean?

To "wolf down" means to eat something very quickly and eagerly. It suggests that the food is being consumed in a hurried and ravenous manner.

Where does it come from?

The expression "wolf down" has its roots in the 1860s and means to eat rapidly and in large amounts, like a hungry wolf devouring its prey.

How to use it?

"I was so hungry that I wolfed down my dinner in just a few minutes."

TO KICK THE BUCKET

What does it mean?

When people say "to kick the bucket," they are referring to dying. The phrase is often used in a casual or informal context, and is one of many idioms used to talk about death in a less serious or somber way.

Where does it come from?

The origin of this idiom most likely comes from the yoke used to hold pigs for slaughter, where their death-throe spasms created the impression of them "kicking the bucket". Another theory is that it relates to suicides who would stand on a large bucket with a noose around the neck and kick away the bucket at the moment of their choosing. The term dates back to at least the 16th century.

How to use it?

"I can't believe that guy kicing the bucket, he was always so full of life."

TO LET THE CAT OUT OF THE BAG

What does it mean?

"To let the cat out of the bag" means to reveal a secret or to share information that was meant to be kept hidden.

Where does it come from?

The origin of the phrase "let the cat out of the bag" is uncertain, but there are two popular theories. One is that it relates to punishment on Navy ships using a whip called a "cat o'nine tails" that was stored in a bag, and revealing the wrongdoing of someone would be like "letting the cat out of the bag". Another theory is about a scam where a customer was sold a cat instead of a suckling pig, and wouldn't know until the bag was opened.

How to use it?

"Don't let the cat out of the bag, or everyone will know our secret plan."

EVERYTHING BUT
THE KITCHEN SINK

What does it mean?

"Everything but the kitchen sink" means including every possible item, or many different things, often more than needed.

Where does it come from?

This phrase originated in the late 19th century as "everything but the kitchen stove." It became popular during World War II when "kitchen sink" was used to describe intense bombardment, meaning "they threw everything at us, even the kitchen sink." It refers to using or including everything in a situation, even the most absurd items.

How to use it?

"Mom packed all of our toys, books, and games in the suitcase for the trip, it was everything but the kitchen sink!"

TO HAVE A CAST IRON STOMACH

What does it mean?

"To have a cast iron stomach" means to have a very strong and tough stomach that can handle eating or drinking anything without getting sick.

Where does it come from?

This expression became popular in the early 1900s, and refers to the toughness and durability of cast iron pans which are used for cooking.

How to use it?

"Tommy has a cast iron stomach. He can eat anything and never gets sick!"

TO USE ONE'S LOAF

What does it mean?

"Use your loaf" is an idiom that means "use your brain" or "think about it carefully". It's like saying "use your head" to make a good decision.

Where does it come from?

This idiom comes from cockney rhyming slang. 'Loaf of bread' equals 'head'.

How to use it?

"If you want to do well in the race, use your loaf and think of a plan before you start running."

DEAD AS A DOORNAIL

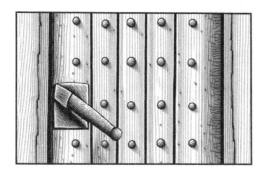

What does it mean?

"Dead as a doornail" means that someone or something is completely dead, without any chance of coming back to life.

Where does it come from?

The phrase comes from the olden days when nails were used to build doors and were pounded in so securely that they could not be pulled out, making them "dead."

How to use it?

"After running a marathon, my legs felt dead as a doornail."

HEAD IN THE CLOUDS

What does it mean?

The phrase "head in the clouds" means that someone is not paying attention to what's happening around them, or that they're not thinking about reality.

Where does it come from?

This saying comes from the 1600s. Back then, people didn't fly in airplanes, so clouds were seen as far away and impossible for people to reach.

How to use it?

Tim always has his head in the clouds, and it's hard for him to stay focused in class.

COOL AS A CUCUMBER

What does it mean?

"Cool as a cucumber" means to be calm and relaxed, like a cucumber which stays cool even in hot weather.

Where does it come from?

The phrase was first recorded in a poem by the British poet John Gay 'New Song on New Similies' in 1732: "Cool as a cucumber could see the rest of womankind".

How to use it?

When the fire alarm went off, Mrs. Smith calmly walked out of the classroom, as cool as a cucumber.

HOLD YOUR HORSES

What does it mean?

"Hold your horses" is an expression used to tell someone to calm down, slow down or be patient.

Where does it come from?

This idiom is believed to have come from horse-racing or from the military, where a horse rider or soldiers were told to control their horses or slow down.

How to use it?

"Hold your horses, Emily! Let's make sure we have all the supplies before we start our project."

OUT OF THE BLUE

What does it mean?

"Out of the blue" means something that happens unexpectedly and without any warning.

Where does it come from?

This idiom is a short for 'out of the clear blue sky', likening a sudden and unexpected event to something unexpectedly falling out of the sky.

How to use it?

"I got a surprise birthday party out of the blue from my friends."

RAINING CATS AND DOGS

What does it mean?

"Raining cats and dogs" is an expression that means it is raining very heavily. It's an old-fashioned phrase that has been used for many years.

Where does it come from?

Back in Old England city streets were dirty and when it rained really hard, dead animals would sometimes get washed away in the rain. Also, cats and dogs both have ancient associations with bad weather.

How to use it?

"Take an umbrella, it seems like it's raining cats and dogs out there."

CAT GOT YOUR TONGUE

What does it mean?

"Cat got your tongue" is a phrase that people use when they think someone is quiet or not saying anything. It's like asking, "Why aren't you talking?"

Where does it come from?

The phrase "cat got your tongue" actually comes from the cat o' nine tails, a whip used to punish sailors. It became slang for "are you afraid to tell?" because if someone knew a secret and told it, they could be punished with the whip.

How to use it?

Billy was so nervous that he couldn't speak, so his friend asked, "Has the cat got your tongue?"

TO TAKE THE MICKEY

What does it mean?

The phrase "take the mickey" means to make fun of someone, or tease them in a playful way.

Where does it come from?

"Take the mickey" may be an abbreviated form of the Cockney rhyming slang "take the Mickey Bliss", a euphemism for "take the piss."

How to use it?

"Don't take the mickey out of your friend for not knowing the answer, it's not nice."

IT'S ALL GREEK TO ME

What does it mean?

"It's all Greek to me" means that something is very difficult to understand or seems like a foreign language.

Where does it come from?

This expression was coined by Shakespeare, who used it literally in Julius Caesar (1:2), where Casca says of a speech by Seneca, deliberately given in Greek so that some would not understand it, "For mine own part, it was Greek to me." It soon was transferred to anything unintelligible.

How to use it?

"Mom, this math problem is all Greek to me!"

PARDON MY FRENCH

What does it mean?

"Pardon my French" is a saying people use when they accidentally say a bad word or a curse word. It's like saying "excuse me" for using a rude word.

Where does it come from?

"Pardon my French" means saying sorry for using a fancy word in a language that may not be understood by the listener. It started as a joke against French people by the English who had a long history of conflict, but now it's just a saying.

How to use it?

"Pardon my French, but I need to explain this problem using big words."

TO BE ON THE BALL

What does it mean?

"To be on the ball" means to be alert, prepared, and ready for anything.

Where does it come from?

The origin of the phrase "to be on the ball" is unclear, but it is thought to have originated in the early 20th century. It likely comes from the sport of baseball, where being "on the ball" meant being aware of the game and ready to make a play.

How to use it?

"My little brother is always on the ball, he never misses anything!"

TO JUMP ON THE BANDWAGON

What does it mean?

"To jump on the bandwagon" means to start doing something because lots of other people are doing it, without really thinking about it for yourself.

Where does it come from?

The phrase "to jump on the bandwagon" originated in the United States in the 19th century and was used to describe people who followed political campaigns. During that time, actual parade wagons with bands were used to travel from town to town to promote political candidates. People would often join the parade and show their support for the candidate by jumping on the bandwagon.

How to use it?

"The new dance craze is so fun, I couldn't resist jumping on the bandwagon and learning the steps."

UNDER THE WEATHER

What does it mean?

"Under the weather" means feeling a little bit sick, not feeling 100% healthy, or having a temporary illness. It's like when the weather outside is cloudy and gray, you might not feel your best either.

Where does it come from?

This idiom has its roots in maritime language. When a sailor became ill or seasick, often because of violent weather conditions, that sailor was sent below decks to the most stable part of the ship, which was under the weather rail. The phrase under the weather rail was shortened to the idiom "under the weather".

How to use it?

"I'm feeling a bit under the weather today, I think I need to rest."

NECK OF THE WOODS

What does it mean?

"Neck of the woods" is a way of saying "a certain area or neighborhood."

Where does it come from?

This idiom is thought to have originated in rural areas of the United States in the 19th century. In those days, forests and woodland areas were divided into smaller sections, and each section was called a "neck." The idea of a "neck" separating different parts of a forest is still used today to describe a narrow area that separates different places or regions.

How to use it?

"Do you know any good ice cream shops in this neck of the woods?"

THICK AS THIEVES

What does it mean?

"Thick as thieves" is an expression that means two or more people are very close friends, or they have a strong bond and trust each other.

Where does it come from?

The idiom "thick as thieves" is a translation of the French idiom "s'entendre comme larron en foire" which in English means "like thieves at a fair." The French phrase means to be complicit with another in an activity which may or may not be lawful.

How to use it?

"My little brother and I are thick as thieves, we stick together no matter what."

TO THROW A SPANNER IN THE WORKS

What does it mean?

"To throw a spanner in the works" means to cause a problem or an obstacle that stops something from working smoothly or successfully.

Where does it come from?

This idiom possibly comes from 1800s when some workers were worried about machines taking their jobs. Some of them would damage the machines by throwing spanners in them to stop them from working.

How to use it?

"We were almost done building the sandcastle on the beach, but a sudden wave threw a wrench in the works and washed it away."

POT CALLING THE KETTLE BLACK

What does it mean?

The phrase "the pot calling the kettle black" is used when someone criticizes another person for something that they themselves are also guilty of doing.

Where does it come from?

The idiom "the pot calling the kettle black" comes from a Spanish novel called Don Quixote. It comes from a time when pots and kettles were made of metal and often became black from soot and smoke when used for cooking over a fire. When one pot criticized the other for being black, it was seen as hypocritical and ridiculous, as both pots would likely have become black from being used in the same way.

How to use it?

"When you say your brother is messy, that's the pot calling the kettle black. Look at how messy your room is!"

TO PUT A SOCK IN IT

What does it mean?

"To put a sock in it" means to be quiet or stop talking. It's like asking someone to stuff a sock in their mouth to muffle their voice. This phrase is often used when someone is talking too much or saying something that is not helpful or wanted.

Where does it come from?

There are two theories about the origin of this idiom: one is that it refers to people stuffing a sock into early gramophones to quieten the music in the absence of a volume control. The more likely origin, however, is from the trenches of the First World War, when it was used by soldiers, along with "put a bung in it" and "put a cork in it" to mean "shut up".

How to use it?

"Can you please put a sock in it? I'm trying to watch a movie!"

COLD TURKEY

What does it mean?

"Cold turkey" means to stop using something suddenly and completely, especially a drug or an addiction.

Where does it come from?

The origin of the phrase "cold turkey" comes from the physical appearance of someone who is abruptly stopping the use of drugs, especially opiates. When an opiate user stops taking the drug, they experience withdrawal symptoms that cause the skin to resemble the scaly, goose-bumped appearance of a cold turkey.

How to use it?

"I might go cold turkey and stop playing video games altogether. I'm really lagging behind at school."

THE ELEPHANT IN THE ROOM

What does it mean?

The phrase "the elephant in the room" is used to describe a situation where there's a big, obvious problem that everyone knows about but nobody wants to talk about or acknowledge. It's like there's a big elephant standing in the middle of the room and everyone is pretending not to see it.

Where does it come from?

The phrase "the elephant in the room" comes from a story written by a poet named Ivan Krylov back in 1814. The story was about a man who goes to a museum and notices all sorts of tiny things, but fails to notice an elephant. The phrase became proverbial.

How to use it?

"Hey, let's talk about the elephant in the room - why didn't we get invited to Sarah's birthday party?"

TO GET SOMEONE'S GOAT

What does it mean?

"To get someone's goat" means to annoy or upset someone. It's like when a goat gets taken away from its owner and it makes him upset.

Where does it come from?

The exact origin of the phrase is not clear, but it may be derived from French "prendre la chèvre" (literally "to take the goat"), or refer to the stealing of a goat mascot from a military unit, etc.

How to use it?

"Don't let Billy get your goat!
Stay calm and keep playing the game."

TO HAVE (OR GET) YOUR DUCKS IN A ROW

What does it mean?

"Having your ducks in a row" means having everything organized and ready to go.

Where does it come from?

The most popular theory suggests that "ducks in a row" came from the world of sports, specifically bowling. Early bowling pins were often shorter and thicker than modern pins, which led to the nickname ducks. Another theory suggests that the idiom "ducks in a row" comes from ship building. A duck is a device that holds the keel in place while building a ship. The first step in building a ship is to get the ducks in straight row thus ensuring a straight keel.

How to use it?

"Let's make sure we have all our ducks in a row before we start our project."

EAGER BEAVER

What does it mean?

An "eager beaver" is someone who is very excited and enthusiastic about doing something. They can't wait to get started and are full of energy!

Where does it come from?

This expression gained its popularity in the U.S. armed forces during WW2, and that it originally referred to a soldier who was excited to impress his superiors by performing duties that others would not like to do.

How to use it?

"Tommy is such an eager beaver, he's always the first one to raise his hand in class!"

TO RUN AROUND LIKE A HEADLESS CHICKEN

What does it mean?

"To run around like a headless chicken" means to act in a panicked or confused way, like a chicken that has lost its head and is running around wildly. It's used to describe someone who is very busy and not sure what they're doing.

Where does it come from?

This idiom comes from medieval England when chickens were popularly killed by chopping off their heads with an axe. Some of the chickens ran around in a panic, crashing into objects after their heads have been chopped off, just before they dropped dead.

How to use it?

"Don't run around like a headless chicken, let's stay calm and think things through."

THE TAIL WAGGING THE DOG

What does it mean?

The phrase "the tail wagging the dog" means that a smaller or less important part of something is having too much control or influence over the whole thing.

Where does it come from?

The phrase originates in the saying "a dog is smarter than its tail, but if the tail were smarter, then it would wag the dog." It is often used in regards to politics.

How to use it?

"Don't let the tail wag the dog, make sure you're in charge and don't let the kids boss you around!"

SACRED COW

What does it mean?

A "Sacred Cow" is an idea or a thing that people consider too important or special to be criticized or changed, sometimes regardless of its worth or validity.

Where does it come from?

The origin of the phrase "sacred cow" comes from Hinduism, where cows are considered sacred and worshipped as symbols of wealth, strength, and motherly love.

How to use it?

"Mike treats his jeans like a sacred cow. They are old and worn out but he won't let me get rid of them."

COCK AND BULL STORY

What does it mean?

A "cock and bull story" is a silly or unbelievable story, often made up just for fun or to trick someone.

Where does it come from?

In 17th century England people traveling between London and Birmingham would stop at two inns called "The Cock" and "The Bull". They would tell tall tales and make up stories that were too wild to be true. These stories became known as a "cock-and-bull stories."

How to use it?

"My little brother said he saw a flying dragon, but I think it's just another one of his cock and bull stories."

MORE HOLES THAN SWISS CHEESE

What does it mean?

This idiom means that something is full of mistakes or has many problems.

Where does it come from?

The origin of this idiom is not clear, but it may come from the fact that Swiss cheese is known for having many holes, or "eyes."

How to use it?

"This plan of yours has more holes than Swiss cheese, let's think of a better idea."

BEST THING SINCE SLICED BREAD

What does it mean?

The phrase "best thing since sliced bread" means that something is very good or excellent.

Where does it come from?

The idiom "best thing since sliced bread" originated from an advertising slogan used by the Chillicothe Baking Company in 1928. This company was the first to sell sliced bread and they used the slogan to promote it as a major innovation in the baking industry. The slogan stated that the introduction of sliced bread was "the greatest forward step in the baking industry since bread was wrapped."

How to use it?

"This new remote control toy is the best thing since sliced bread. I can't wait to play it with my friend!"

TO BEEF UP

What does it mean?

"To beef up" means to make something stronger or more powerful.

Where does it come from?

The idiom "to beef up" originated as college slang. It comes from the word "beef," which means muscle-power.

How to use it?

"Let's beef up our lemonade stand by adding some decorations and signs to make it look more attractive."

TO GO BANANAS

What does it mean?

The phrase "to go bananas" means to become very excited, crazy, or upset.

Where does it come from?

"The phrase ""to go bananas"" has its roots in American college campuses in the 1960s. It evolved from the idiom ""going ape,"" which also means to go crazy, to explode with anger, or to erupt with enthusiasm.

How to use it?

"Sophie went bananas when she heard she won the prize in the raffle."

TO HAVE A BONE TO PICK WITH SOMEONE

What does it mean?

"To have a bone to pick with someone" means to have a disagreement or problem with someone that you want to talk about and resolve.

Where does it come from?

The phrase "to have a bone to pick with someone" comes from the 16th century and is based on the idea of two dogs fighting over a bone.

How to use it?

"Mom, I have a bone to pick with you. You promised we could go to the park this Sunday and you're telling me that we're not going."

TO TAKE SOMETHING WITH A GRAIN (OR PINCH) OF SALT

What does it mean?

The phrase "to take something with a grain of salt" means to not believe something completely and to be a bit skeptical or cautious about it.

Where does it come from?

The phrase "to take something with a grain of salt" has a long history, with some beliefs tracing it back to ancient times to Pliny the Elder in 77 A.D. The phrase originally came from the idea of adding a grain of salt to an antidote for poison to make it more effective.

How to use it?

"My little brother said he saw a unicorn in the backyard, but I take that with a grain of salt because I don't think unicorns are real."

PIE IN THE SKY

What does it mean?

The phrase "pie in the sky" means something that is not realistic or achievable. When people talk about "pie in the sky" ideas or plans, they mean that they are not practical or likely to happen.

Where does it come from?

The phrase "pie in the sky" originated from a song called "The Preacher and the Slave" written by labor activist Joe Hill in 1911. The song was a parody of a Salvation Army hymn and criticized the organization for only focusing on people's spiritual needs rather than their practical ones.

How to use it?

"I wish I could have a million toys, but that's just pie in the sky."

TO GET UP ON THE WRONG SIDE OF THE BED

What does it mean?

"To get up on the wrong side of the bed" means to have a bad mood or to feel grumpy for no particular reason.

Where does it come from?

The origin of the expression 'wake up on the wrong side of the bed' is thought to come from ancient Rome. Romans were very careful always to get up on the correct side of the bed to ensure that good luck would follow them through their days.

How to use it?

"My sister is being so grumpy today, I think she must have gotten up on the wrong side of the bed."

TO PULL THE WOOL OVER SOMEONE'S EYES

What does it mean?

"To pull the wool over someone's eyes" means to trick or deceive someone, to make them believe something that is not true.

Where does it come from?

The phrase "to pull the wool over someone's eyes" might have its roots in medieval fairs where robbers would trick their victims. They would pull their hood over their eyes and steal from them. This idea of covering someone's eyes to deceive them gave rise to the expressions "to pull the wool over someone's eyes" and "to hoodwink".

How to use it?

"When my little brother says he's not hungry, I know he's trying to pull the wool over my eyes."

BY THE SKIN OF YOUR TEETH

What does it mean?

"By the skin of your teeth" is an expression that means you barely made it or just escaped something by a very close margin.

Where does it come from?

This phrase comes from the Bible. In Job 19:20, the King James Version of the Bible says, "My bone cleaveth to my skin and to my flesh, and I am escaped by the skin of my teeth." In the Geneva Bible, the phrase is rendered as "I have escaped with the skinne of my tethe."

How to use it?

"I barely made it to school on time. I escaped being late by the skin of my teeth!"

TO GO BELLY UP

What does it mean?

"To go belly up" means to fail or stop working properly. It is also a way of saying that something has come to an end.

Where does it come from?

The phrase "to go belly up" comes from the idea of a dead fish or animal floating upside down in the water with its belly facing up.

How to use it?

"If you don't work hard in school, your grades might go belly up and you won't get into a good college."

ARMED TO THE TEETH

What does it mean?

"Armed to the teeth" means that someone has a lot of weapons and is ready to use them. It means they are prepared for a fight or dangerous situation.

Where does it come from?

This idiom originates in the 14th century, when knights often wore head-to-foot armor. The idiom, however, only gained currency in the mid-1800s, at first still applied to weapons or other military equipment. Today it is used still more figuratively.

How to use it?

"If you're going on a camping trip, make sure you're armed to the teeth with all the right gear, like a tent, sleeping bag, and cooking supplies."

TO BURST AT THE SEAMS

What does it mean?

When something is so full, it might be about to burst open.

Where does it come from?

This expression started to become popular in the 1800s. It is related to the seams in fabric. A seam is where two pieces of fabric are sewn together. If a bag is very full, the seams will begin to bulge apart from the pressure.

How to use it?

"You've got so many books, your backpack is about to burst at the seams!"

FAT CHANCE

What does it mean?

"Fat chance" means a very small chance or a very unlikely possibility. It's like saying "there's not much hope for that to happen".

Where does it come from?

The phrase "fat chance" probably started as a joke, with people using the word "fat" as a sarcastic version of saying "slim chance".

How to use it?

"Do you think you'll win the school contest? Fat chance!"

TO PICK ONE'S BRAIN

What does it mean?

"To pick one's brain" means to ask someone for their ideas or thoughts on a subject.

Where does it come from?

The expression "to pick one's brain" has been used since the mid-1800s and refers to the act of trying to learn or gather information from someone. The phrase comes from the idea of picking clean the bones of an animal.

How to use it?

"My little sister wants to pick my brain about how to solve the math problem she's stuck on."

TO GO DOWN THE RABBIT HOLE

What does it mean?

"To go down the rabbit hole" means to go on an unexpected journey or enter into a strange, confusing, or unpredictable situation.

Where does it come from?

This idiom comes from the story of Alice in Wonderland, where Alice follows a rabbit into a hole and finds herself in a strange and wonderful world.

How to use it?

When Sarah opened the mysterious door, she felt like she was going down the rabbit hole.

TO FLY OFF THE HANDLE

What does it mean?

"To fly off the handle" means to become very angry
or excited and lose control of your emotions.

Where does it come from?

"Fly off the Handle" is an American phrase that
alludes to the way that an axe head can fly off its
handle if it becomes loose.

How to use it?

Jimmy was feeling so frustrated with his math
homework that he started to fly off the handle and
yell at the book.

TO BE IN A PICKLE

What does it mean?

"To be in a pickle" means to be in a difficult or confusing situation.

Where does it come from?

This idiom is thought to come from two different origins, one being the sixteenth century Dutch phrase "in de pekel zitten" which means "sitting in the pickle" and refers to being drunk. Another origin is from Shakespeare's play The Tempest, in which a character says "How camest thou in this pickle?" referring to being drunk, and eventually the phrase came to mean to be in a difficult situation.

How to use it?

"I promised to bring cupcakes for the school bake sale, but I totally forgot about it. I'm in a real pickle now."

STORM IN A TEACUP

What does it mean?

"Storm in a teacup" means making a big fuss over something small or unimportant.

Where does it come from?

This phrase has been used for centuries and is similar in other languages, including French and Latin. The sentiment of a tempest in a teapot can be traced back to ancient Rome, where Cicero used a similar phrase to describe making a big deal over something small.

How to use it?

"Mom, I don't know why Timmy is making such a storm in a teacup about me eating the last cookie. There's more of them in the pantry."

I COULD EAT A HORSE

What does it mean?

"I could eat a horse" means that someone is very, very hungry. It's just a saying and nobody would actually eat a horse! It just means they have a big appetite and would like to eat a lot of food.

Where does it come from?

This phrase has been used since the 19th century, but it's not exactly known where it came from. But, it might have started because people were so hungry they thought they could even eat a big animal like a horse.

How to use it?

"I was so hungry during the camping trip, I felt like I could eat a horse!" said Jake.

TO BEAT AROUND THE BUSH

What does it mean?

When someone is "beating around the bush", it means that they are not speaking directly about a certain topic or are avoiding answering a question directly.

Where does it come from?

This idiom came about through bird hunting when participants used to beat bushes to stir the birds from them while others caught them in nets. So, 'beating about the bush' was the start of the actual capture, but not the end result.

How to use it?

When I asked Sarah what she wanted for her birthday, she kept beating around the bush and wouldn't give me a straight answer.

BOB'S YOUR UNCLE

What does it mean?

"Bob's your uncle" is an expression used to mean "and there you have it" or "it's that simple." It's often used to make things sound easier or more straightforward than they might seem.

Where does it come from?

In 1887, British Prime Minister Robert Gascoyne-Cecil appointed his nephew Arthur James Balfour as Minister for Ireland. The phrase 'Bob's your uncle' was coined when Arthur referred to the Prime Minister as 'Uncle Bob'. Apparently, it's very simple to become a minister when Bob's your uncle!

How to use it?

"Building a fort is easy, just grab some blankets, chairs, and Bob's your uncle, you have a cozy hideout!"

FROG IN YOUR THROAT

What does it mean?

"Frog in your throat" means when your voice sounds hoarse, rough or croaky like a frog. It can happen when your throat is sore, or you have a cold.

Where does it come from?

The expression to have a frog in one's throat first appeared in the United States during the 1800s, and comes from the fact that a person so afflicted sounds as if he is croaking like a frog. All other stories floating around the internet about frogs being a medieval cure for various maladies is apocryphal.

How to use it?

"I don't think I can sing today,
I feel like I have a frog in my throat."

TO KEEP ONE'S EYES PEELED

What does it mean?

"To keep one's eyes peeled" means to be very watchful and alert.

Where does it come from?

The expression "to keep your eyes peeled" comes from the idea of peeling back the skin of your eyelids so you can see better. This helps you be more aware and prepared for what's around you. The expression has been used since the 1800s.

How to use it?

"If you want to catch the ice cream truck, you better keep your eyes peeled!"

TO KEEP ONE'S SHIRT ON

What does it mean?

"To keep one's shirt on" means to stay calm and not get too upset or angry about something.

Where does it come from?

This idiom started in 1800s in America when men didn't have many shirts to wear. They would take off their shirt before getting into a fight so it wouldn't get ruined or dirty. That's where the saying comes from.

How to use it?

When you're playing a sport, it's important to keep your shirt on and not let your temper get the best of you.

TO POUR YOUR HEART OUT/INTO (SOMETHING)

What does it mean?

"To pour your heart into something" means to put a lot of effort, time, and emotion into doing something you care about.

Where does it come from?

The phrase "to pour your heart into something" comes from a verse in the Bible. In Psalms 62:8, it says "Trust in him at all times; ye people, pour out your heart before him: God is a refuge for us."

How to use it?

Sarah pours her heart into her music, playing the piano with all her soul.

TO CALL DIBS

What does it mean?

"To call dibs" means to say that you want something before anyone else does, and you want it to be yours. It's like saying "I want that toy first!" or "I want to sit in the front seat!" By calling dibs, you're claiming the thing you want so that no one else can have it.

Where does it come from?

The origin of "to call dibs" comes from a children's game called dibstones that was played a long time ago. In the game, players would "dab" or "pat" something to claim it as theirs. Over time, kids started using the phrase "to call dibs" to mean claiming something for themselves. Nowadays, people of all ages still use this phrase to say they want something to be theirs.

How to use it?

"I call dibs on that last slice of pizza!"

TO THROW (SOMEONE) A BONE

What does it mean?

"To throw someone a bone" means to give them a small piece of help or support.

Where does it come from?

This idiom comes from the idea of giving a dog a bone to keep them quiet or happy. The point is simply to quiet the dog, not to give him a healthy meal that is good for him. The exact origin of this expression is not known, but it has been used for a long time!

How to use it?

The teacher threw us a bone and gave us an extra five minutes for recess.

TO BE OUT OF THE FRYING PAN AND INTO THE FIRE

What does it mean?

"To be out of the frying pan and into the fire" means to go from a bad situation to an even worse one.

Where does it come from?

One of the earliest known uses of this idiom may be from Sir Thomas More in A Dialogue Concerning Heresies, first published in 1529. The phrase is like a picture in your mind, imagining you're slowly cooking in a frying pan and you decide to jump out of it to escape the heat. But, when you jump out, you end up falling into an even bigger fire, which is much worse.

How to use it?

"I thought switching to a different school would solve all my problems, but now I feel like I went from the frying pan into the fire."

TO RING A BELL

What does it mean?

The idiom "to ring a bell" means to bring back a memory or a feeling of recognition.

Where does it come from?

Some people think it comes from a famous experiment done by a scientist named Ivan Pavlov. He worked with dogs and found out that they could remember things if they heard a bell ring.

How to use it?

"I don't remember the name of this actor, but his face is ringing a bell."

TO BLOW OFF STEAM

What does it mean?

To "blow off steam" means to do something to release pent up energy, frustration, or anger.

Where does it come from?

The phrase "to blow off steam" is an old expression that originated from the early days of trains. Back then, trains were powered by steam and if the steam pressure built up too much, it could cause an explosion. To avoid this, engineers would pull a lever to release some of the steam and keep the train safe.

How to use it?

Billy loves to play soccer to blow off steam after a long day at school.

TO CUT TO THE CHASE

What does it mean?

"To cut to the chase" means to get straight to the most important or main part of something, without wasting time on unimportant details.

Where does it come from?

The phrase 'cut to the chase' originated in the American film industry, when many early movies ended in a chase scene. The first printed reference to the expression comes from script direction from the 1929 Hollywood Girl: "Jannings escapes… Cut to the chase."

How to use it?

"I'm in a hurry, can you please cut to the chase and tell me what you want for breakfast?"

TO BE UP IN THE AIR

What does it mean?

"To be up in the air" means to be uncertain or unresolved, like a balloon floating in the air.

Where does it come from?

Some people believe this idiom might have started from the idea of a coin toss. When a coin is tossed, you don't know which side it will land on until it falls back down, just like with a decision that's "up in the air."

How to use it?

"We're still trying to decide where to go on our family vacation, so everything is up in the air right now."

TO GIVE A RUN FOR ONE'S MONEY

What does it mean?

"To give someone a run for their money" means to compete with someone in a way that makes it a close and exciting race or competition.

Where does it come from?

The origin of this phrase is thought to come from horse racing, where people enjoyed watching a close and exciting race even if they didn't win any money.

How to use it?

"My little brother is getting better at chess, he'll soon give me a run for my money!"

TO BREAK THE BANK

What does it mean?

"To break the bank" means to use all of your money or to spend so much that you have no more money left.

Where does it come from?

This term originated sometime around 1600, when gamblers won more money than the house (bank) could afford to pay.

How to use it?

We don't want to break the bank, so let's choose a cheaper restaurant for dinner.

TO MAKE ENDS MEET

What does it mean?

"To make ends meet" means having enough money to pay for all the things you need, like food, a place to live, and clothes.

Where does it come from?

This idiom probably originally referred to the ends of rope meeting, signifying continuity and therefore security and stability. Perhaps shifting later to refer to the attempt at making money last from one pay period to the next (i.e. the ends), thereby leaving no gap or break in the availability of funds.

How to use it?

Sarah has to work extra hours so she can make ends meet and pay her bills on time.

RULE OF THUMB

What does it mean?

A "rule of thumb" is an old saying that gives a simple way to remember how to do something. It's kind of like a shortcut that helps people make a quick decision or solve a problem.

Where does it come from?

One theory is that it comes from the practice of using one's thumb as a rough guide for measurement. Another theory is that it comes from the idea that a husband could legally beat his wife with a stick as long as it was no thicker than his thumb. However, these theories are disputed and the exact origin remains unclear.

How to use it?

As a rule of thumb, you should always eat breakfast before going to school.

TO FIND ONE'S FEET

What does it mean?

"To find one's feet" means to start feeling comfortable and confident in a new situation or environment.

Where does it come from?

This phrase has been in around in various forms sine ancient times, but the origin is not known. However, it is believed that it refers to newborns (humans and animals) standing up and starting to walk.

How to use it?

When Mary started at her new school, it took her some time to find her feet, but she soon made lots of friends.

TO COMPARE APPLES AND ORANGES

What does it mean?

The phrase "to compare apples and oranges" means to compare two things that are very different and cannot be compared fairly.

Where does it come from?

The phrase "comparing apples to oranges" comes from a collection of proverbs from 1670. It originally said "apples to oysters" but changed over time.

How to use it?

"It's not fair to compare your toy car to my doll, they're apples and oranges."

NOT ONE'S CUP OF TEA

What does it mean?

"Not one's cup of tea" means that something is not to one's liking or interest. It's like saying "I don't like it" or "it's not for me".

Where does it come from?

The origin of the phrase "not one's cup of tea" can be traced back to World War II. Back then, people started using this phrase to mean that they didn't like someone very much. Before the war, the phrase "my cup of tea" was used to describe a favored friend, especially one with a lively and enjoyable personality.

How to use it?

"Jenny doesn't like going to amusement parks, it's not her cup of tea."

TO SPILL THE BEANS

What does it mean?

When someone "spills the beans," it means they have told a secret or revealed important information that was supposed to be kept quiet.

Where does it come from?

The origin of "to spill the beans" comes from ancient Greece. They used to have a special way of voting for leaders. They would put either a white bean (for yes) or a brown bean (for no) in a jar, and the votes would be kept secret. But if the jar was bumped and the beans spilled out, everyone would know how the people voted.

How to use it?

"I almost spilled the beans about my sister's birthday present, but I stopped myself just in time."

TO PULL SOMEONE'S LEG

What does it mean?

"To pull someone's leg" means to play a trick or joke on someone by telling them something that is not true, in a teasing or playful way.

Where does it come from?

The phrase comes from Scotland and it used to mean making a fool of someone by cheating them. One theory is that it started from pulling someone's leg to trip them, making them look silly.

How to use it?

"When my dad said he saw a bear in our backyard, I knew he was just pulling my leg."

BREAD AND BUTTER

What does it mean?

"Bread and butter" means the basic things that someone needs to live or the main source of someone's income.

Where does it come from?

The expression "bread and butter" originates from the 1700s. The original definition of the phrase meant your basic needs to sustain yourself. The phrase changed its meaning during the 1800s to refer to a person's livelihood or income.

How to use it?

"Earning money from selling ice cream at the park is my bread and butter at the moment."

SALT OF THE EARTH

What does it mean?

"Salt of the earth" is a phrase that is used to describe people who are honest, kind, hardworking, and good-hearted.

Where does it come from?

The phrase derives from Jesus' Sermon on the Mount: "You are the salt of the earth." (Matthew 5:13) Jesus meant that the common people he was addressing — fishermen, shepherds, laborers — were worthy and virtuous. He was alluding, not to the tang of salt, but to its value.

How to use it?

"Our teacher is the salt of the earth, always making learning fun and being there for us."

BETWEEN A ROCK AND A HARD PLACE

What does it mean?

When someone is in a situation where they have two difficult choices and can't decide what to do, we say that they are "between a rock and a hard place". It means they are stuck in a difficult situation and can't find an easy solution.

Where does it come from?

In Homer's Odyssey, Odysseus must pass between Charybdis, a treacherous whirlpool, and Scylla, a horrid man-eating, cliff-dwelling monster. Ever since, saying one is stuck between a rock (the cliff) and a hard place (the whirlpool) has been a way to succinctly describe being in a dilemma.

How to use it?

"Two of my best friends had a fight and I can't make up my mind whose side I'm on. I'm caught between a rock and a hard place."

TO BE OFF THE HOOK

What does it mean?

When you say someone is "off the hook," it means they are no longer in trouble or in a difficult situation.

Where does it come from?

This idiom originated from fishing, where you catch fish with a hook. A fish that has been caught is considered on the hook and out of options. But it can escape or be off the hook.

How to use it?

Susan promised to clean her room, but she forgot. When her dad said it was okay, she was finally off the hook.

ONCE IN A BLUE MOON

What does it mean?

"Once in a blue moon" means something that happens very rarely or hardly ever.

Where does it come from?

The origin of the idiom "once in a blue moon" is uncertain, but it is thought to come from the rare occurrence of a second full moon within a calendar month, which appears blue in color.

How to use it?

"Once in a blue moon I get to go to the movies, when there's a film I really want to watch."

TO THROW IN THE TOWEL

What does it mean?

The phrase "to throw in the towel" means to give up or quit trying.

Where does it come from?

This idiom comes from boxing, where a cornerman (a person who helps a boxer) would throw a towel into the ring to signal that the fighter they were helping has quit and the match is over.

How to use it?

Timmy's team was behind in the basketball game, but they refused to throw in the towel. They worked together and made a comeback to win the game!

AT THE DROP OF A HAT

What does it mean?

"At the drop of a hat" means to do something immediately or very quickly, without needing much time to prepare.

Where does it come from?

This idiom originates in the 19th century. It was common then to signal the beginning of a fight or race by either dropping a hat or sweeping it in a rapid downward motion.

How to use it?

"If my best friend asks me to come play, I'll leave everything and go with her at the drop of a hat."

TO LET SLEEPING DOGS LIE

What does it mean?

"To let sleeping dogs lie" means not to disturb or mess with something that is currently calm or peaceful.

Where does it come from?

This idiom comes from Geoffrey Chaucer's poem Troilus and Criseyde, published in 1374. The original phrase was "It is nought good a sleping hound to wake."

How to use it?

"Mom, can we not talk about my grades from last semester? Let's just let sleeping dogs lie."

TO BE ON THE FENCE

What does it mean?

When someone is "on the fence," they're having trouble making a decision. They're not sure what to do and are considering two or more choices, but can't pick one.

Where does it come from?

This phrase refers to someone who can't make up their mind, just like they're sitting on a fence and can't decide which way to go. The idea is that someone who is "on the fence" is not making a choice, but instead is in a neutral or undecided position.

How to use it?

"Sophie's parents are on the fence about letting her get a pet, so she has to keep convincing them it's a good idea."

THANK YOU!

Thank you for choosing to explore the world of idioms with us. We hope that this book has been an enjoyable and educational journey for you, filled with fun and fascinating phrases.

We value your feedback and would appreciate if you could take a moment to share your thoughts on the book, whether by leaving a review on the site where you purchased it or by emailing us directly at: lilas.publishing@ya.ru.

Your opinion matters to us as we strive to improve and create the best possible content for our readers! Thank you again for your support!

Printed in Great Britain
by Amazon